MOVING STILLNESS

haiku by

David Samuel Bloch

illustration by

Julie Hagan Bloch

AHA Books

MOVING STILLNESS
Written by David Samuel Bloch
Haiku Copyright © 1999 David Samuel Bloch
Relief Print Illustration by Julie Hagan Bloch
Illustration Copyright © 1999 Julie Hagan Bloch

Editorial Advice
by Alice Bloch and Jane Reichhold

ISBN: 0-944-676-84-7
Library of Congress: 99-64615

Published and Distributed by:
AHA Books
POB 1250
Gualala, CA 95445
USA

Also distributed by:
Julie Bloch
R.D. 1, Box 9A
Hurleyville, NY 12747
USA

MOVING STILLNESS

David Samuel Bloch

Haiku

Julie Hagan Bloch

Illustration

Dedication

To that most healing,
deepest feeling, sacred source
of the universe

Our gratitude goes out to:

Alice Bloch, for the input of her insight-filled intellect, her always honest appraisal and clarity of communication; Roz Stendahl, for her support, in the form of perfectly-timed provision of materials and nourishment of spirit; "Uncle Walter" Israel, for his contribution of all carving blocks used in print preparation; Jane Reichhold, for her faith in and patience with us, her constant, wise counsel, her willingness to interact from the heart, and her proven publishing expertise; all of the individuals (you know who you are) too numerous to name, but who have encouraged us and urged us on with their loving support.

CONTENTS

Little Miracles

Dedication

To You who have so well concealed
in the mundane
the miraculous

Response of the heart
      to a woodpecker's knocking
          —opening of spring

Vernal Equinox —
      cover of snow can't conceal
          Earth's celebration

Mid-April sun, you've missed some...
      ice on the lake,
          snow on the forest floor

Raindrops make bookmarks,
      tug the attention from the written
          to the real

Main Street signs creaking
      —won't somebody tune them up
          before the parade

Spring dawn — a solid circle of ice
from the dog's outdoor dish
flipped out!

Around the bend glimpse —
hind hooves leave the ground... vanish
into the thicket

Pent-up steam
piping hot music in
—calliope percolator

Lots of dots...
dearth of dashes
—woodpecker's Morse-encoded messages

High winds have me holding my breath
—our own leaning tower
of hemlock

The wind registers
    its every move with willows
       planted in mud

Sky Chef, it's scrumptious!
    —this scrambled sunset sandwich
       cloudy evening snack

Curtain of haze — clouds step out
    ham it up in the spotlight
       of the sun

A day's work to be done
    up-early woodpeckers
       already at it

Wakeful, I wonder
    how long he's been hammering
       away at my sleep

Storm warnings sent out
        over the open airwaves
                —thunder's rumblings

Driving rain — wonder what became
        of that frog who jumped
                into traffic

Darkness wrapped in a sheet of rain —
        white, night lightning
                ripped that shroud to shreds

River rock-hopping —
        on my shoulder hitching a ride,
                dragonfly guide

Middle of May — coming into bloom,
        the old crab apple
                piñata

You can tell they've had enough to drink —
fruit trees all bloated
with blossoms

A bandstand in our backyard —
blaring orange trumpet vine
flourishes

In such proximity
so much variation
—columbine in bloom

A whole bloomin' bunch
of color combinations
—little miracles

Burying the dead woodpecker —
I think someone should be sounding
Taps

Wind breaks the news: spring's passing
       visibly shaken —
              blossoms from branches

Given keys to wind and earth —
     a generation of maples
                    gets wings

Exposed — tree roots reporting
     lawn mower assaults
               countless, the clippings

Prominent rib cage —
     half the neighborhood feeds the dog
                    feeding his worms

The bark of the tree
     biting the barbed wire back
   —trapped, the trespasser

Dog walk in progress —
     through the lattice... pokes... the nose
               of the next to go

Lifting up the screen
    to experience today
        as it really is

High honors!
    It's been draped all over the mountain —
        a wreath of laurel

Refreshment needed...
    the lawn mower serves it up
        —a cool whiff of mint

Garter snake,
    you're not unwelcome here — it's just that
        your home needs mowing

To think I was prematurely born
    —always saying,
            "Sorry, I'm late"

His longing to play
    frees the puppy from his chain
        —Independence Day

Can't put my finger
    on that which the goldfinch grasps
        —prickle of thistle

The side yard as seen
    through lattice-covered windows
        —each square is complete

Bye-bye blueberries!
  —but in purple on my tongue...
dyeing, you live on

Urban scrawl, the wall of a bridge
    spanning the spectrum
           signed ROY G BIV

The goldfish gone...
   turtles, carp about the pond
   —lost, some local color

Kaleidoscope — churned contents
            of the mind — looking
                for a new design

The mess on my desk
   becomes a work of art
         through the kaleidoscope

Mist materializing
         another dimension
               in the meadow

Water balloon fight —
   drenched, declared-noncombatant
            steaming in the sun

Chicory and Queen Anne's Lace
—my attention
a divided highway

You stream-top raindrops
can't fool me — I know really
you're water striders

Japanese beetles —
roses and I implore you:
mind your mandibles!

Bicycle riding —
as everything passes,
no worries today

Last year's leftovers
or this fall's appetizers?
—browned bunches of leaves

One small step for a man
                    with mower,
   ...one giant leap for cricketkind!

Frog escapes the mower blade
                 in the nick of time
   —close shave, Uncle Dave!

Birds in a blanket
         sample surfacing earthworms
   —countdown to downpour

The wind picking up,
      and I also...
   the scent of the approaching storm

Overcast sky
      but for a stunning single spot
         of brilliant blue

Where sunlight sharpens
the dull edge of a dark cloud
—a silver sliver

Surface of a stream —
　　cloud reflections calmly drift
　　　　counter to current

I'm up! — mockingbird
　　perfectly mimics the call
　　　　of my alarm clock

At daybreak a spark
　　　from the burning horizon
　　—clouds catching fire

Of wind not so much
　　　as a whisper through the trees
　—bicycling's a breeze!

Exhilarating!
　　　downhill accelerating
　—fresh air on my face

Getting dark early —
     most painful, the transition
       to the indoor bike

Waitress awaited...
     patron at the piano...
     presto! supper's served

In shadow of swan —
     fish scavenge bits of feast dropped
      by clumsy waders

Ferry's forceful wake —
   a crease-crossing motorboat
   fails to unfold it

Home from the city...
     heavy traffic on our street
      —two cars and a truck

Chickens — how proudly
 they pick through the trash... then squawk
     how slim their pickin's

Stone wall — chipmunk
     makes an appearance in each
         of its crevices

Lawn statuary —
     suddenly one of those geese
 had the nerve to move!

Crashing through the brush —
         one enormous buck
         wakes up the sleepy hollow

Double the dose of orange
     —autumn foliage
         lit by morning sun

Autumn —
    old dwellings along the way
      falling deeper into decay

In retirement
  letting the farm go to seed
    —fields full of milkweed

Its back nearly broken,
  it can hardly hold up its head
    —sunflower

At the signal from wind chimes —
    trees drip yesterday's raindrops
      on my head

Milkweed, no one else needs to know
    who's offered what
      wishes to the wind

A frayed pair of ropes
        remains of an old tree swing
            —the wind has it sway

Reincarnated,
        rays to rainbows on its spray
    —fountain in full sun

Leaves all waiting...
        —the wind promises to take them
            for one last whirl

Why they look so chewed up —
        canna lilies bitten
                by the first few frosts

Sprinkling on my head...
        through clouds I can just make it out
                    —the Big Dipper

Even out here, haves and have nots —
      some trees full,
            others missing their leaves

Making my Hallowe'en mask myself
   this year... took two weeks...
                  not shaving

Home from Florida —
         willows, last to lose their leaves,
            finish fall for me

Not only not late,
         nearly an hour early!
   —end of DST

End of October,...
         suddenly inspiration kicks in
   —spring cleaning!

Autumn cleaning —
 what it takes sometimes to break the spell
  of inertia

Feeling of fullness —
    from feasting on an orange
        final fall sunrise

An icy footprint —
    the sole survivor of snow
            and subsequent rain

Winter haiku walk —
       layers insulate me
           from my subject matter

Huddled after heeding
      the building's fire bells —
         cold as all get out!

Cloudless, but the sky
      is hardly empty... sun, moon,
         and infinite blue

...And Infinite Blue

Dedication

To You who bring
to each instant, infinite blessings
from out of the blue

How much more bubbly
    seems the stream at each crossing
  —New Year's midnight bridge

Ficus in focus...
    what's this? dancing polka dots?
  —winter ladybug

My mind, take this down
    so we don't slip up again
  —baby steps on ice!

At the open door
    the same dog who begged, now balks
  —chilling winter rain

There's a dog, I swear!
    not just the snow-patched earth there
      —her calico coat

Reciting haiku...
   poised to make a splash, a frog
      jumps... into my throat

How could I swat it?
  a wasp so utterly trapped
  —middle of winter

One command keeps us
  upstanding citizens — "Dogs...
      Easy!" over ice

Full Moon, you've been found
  peeking out from behind them —
     thick curtains of clouds

So reassuring, this glimpse —
  I wonder
    had I doubted you were there

Blizzard predicted —
    what follows is a flurry
  of activity

Midst of a blizzard —
  the airport filled with
    no one going anywhere

Melting rooftop snow —
    just about through the ice, drips
    each mild moment

Spring thaw smells of fall —
    ah, the sun's warming us up
  some leftover leaves

Evergreens in mist —
    amassing moisture enough,
       droplets they let drop

My morning shower —
    only yesterday I ran
  to escape the rain

Grandpa's funeral —
    a gentle-hearted soul lived
  and died — dignified

Prop plane in a lightning storm
    over the Ozarks
       —prayer in the air

Striking!
    the orange light of daybreak upon it —
       robin's sunburst breast

Feline foliage,
    cattails and pussy willows —
      poised with pen, I pounce

Rain, sun... many such showers
        you've sheltered us from,
                great spruce guardian

Tree falls — wind, you've done it!
        homeless birds up in the air
                all aflutter

My giant old friend —
        finally you get to rest
                your crown on the ground

The uprooted tree —
        look out below when you go
                wishing for windfalls

Odd, from the kitchen window —
        tonight, the sight
                of unobstructed sky

The spruce tree's demise —
a new intensity
to our view of sunrise

Shun shallowness, root deep!
　　this thought brought to you
　　　　by a wind-toppled tree

Reflected sunlight
　　reflected again — shining
　　　　moonlit daffodils

The real time of spring —
　　a woodpecker tapping out
　　　　its rapid rhythm

Dank air feel — moist earth smell,
　　gurgling sounds — stream
　　　　all but seen in the dark

Along the trail, now,
　　　　where rails used to run — coal dust
　　　　dissolves the distance

The outermost ring glistening —
    spruce stump
    with its sap pump left running

Mountain ash planted...
    muscles sore, spirits soaring
      —heron overhead

Climbing in the sky...
    heron spreads wings wide,
        catches the current — free ride!

Lights from the local street lamps
    find me in the fog
        circle-encircled

Spruce tree shaken out —
    yellow plume of pollen
      whisked away by the wind

Peony blossom
  lying in the dirt,
  you've lost none of your luster

Safety goggles on,
  he oversees me mowing the lawn
   —dragonfly

The spot you've been staring at
  lights up as you look away
   —fireflies!

Sudden storm — stealing some
   of its thunder, lightning bugs
    flicker through rain

Coming soon: bushy gardens —
  earthworms receive
    free rototiller rides

They'll take care of this site, all right!
   —tent caterpillars
       camped in our trees

Turkey vulture... space...
      as much as it can scavenge
   —its whopping wingspan!

but chipmunk, earthquakes
     come with the territory
       —basketball practice

One blustery day,
   I'm out shooting baskets — ferns,
      the fans, make a wave!

Razor ribbon perch —
    a finch serenades
    the criminally insane

Nothing in your net...
hungry yet? or have you already et?
...spider!

Guy spreading stones
insists, "No poetry in this!"
—gravel in his voice

White ball bounces off...
bunny, wait, don't you want
to help me walk the dogs?

Eager, ten eyes wait...
for the beaver to come out
from under the bridge

Deft strokes —
in still water the beaver has written
an inverted V

Abundance of brush —
    so much astir over so little
                a chipmunk

Rabbit,
    your secret's safe with me
(that your hole is under the mailbox!)

Dusk —
  with the approach of headlights
  the dark shape of a deer... disappears

Exploding into white smoke
    of marshland fog — Queen Anne's Lace,
            croaks of frogs

Concentric circles —
    at the center of each set,
     a water strider

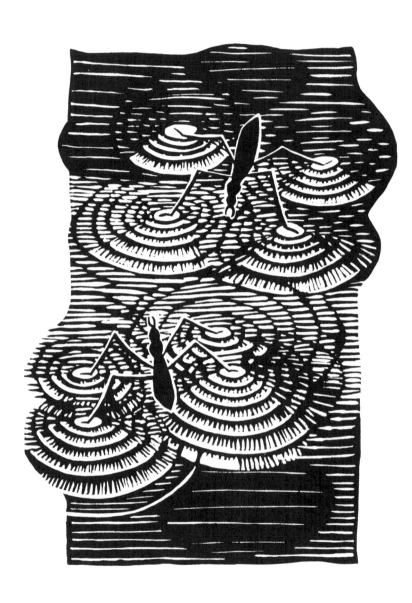

Rings expand and overlap
　　　—water bugs spreading
　their rippled netting

Landlocked... an odd key
        —the lone cry of a seagull
    sweeps me out to sea

Passersby,
        follow my eyes
    to a cloud fully outlined in sunlight

A seagull swoops down...
    and from the manmade lake comes
        the catch of the day

Ceremoniously,
        three ducks parade past
            the hotel swimming pool

Noontime swim —
    on the inside of my goggles, a drop
                        of sunlight

At rainbow's end,
   greater than any pot of gold —
      Niagara Falls

Table Rock Restaurant —
   between sips of coffee,
      drinking in the falls

Spirit of the Falls
      manifests manifold forms —
         wind-shaped, made of mist

Under meteor showers
      dogs walk and fleas jump
         every which way

Almost ninety degrees… I freeze
      … bees!
   —the entire spruce tree buzzing

Over the river, at the bridge —
  a moment there
          mingled with the mist

Eyes, you've only
  to trace the winding trail of mist
     —where the river is!

End-of-summer drought —
          all the forest engulfed
                in silent prayer

Water restrictions —
        suddenly okay to pray out loud
                    for more rain

Autumn coloring...
        faintly at first, filtering
    through the greenery

Remaining bird's call
      fades into the background
            —clamor of fall colors

Ping... ping... what was that?
    couldn't be rain — star-lit sky
        frost-laden leaves... fall!

Wind tumbling through the trees
        flying colors —
                autumn acrobatics

Spread of red
        seed clusters pointed skyward
    —sumac's sunrise silhouette

Five inches of rain, post-drought,
        overnight swells
                the river to a roar

An intimate table for two —
    through the window...
        climbing, the full moon!

Lavender everywhere
    but there — evergreens
        shading the mountain

Sixty degrees —
    an unexpected extra bit of spring
        in my step

Off to the thrift store —
    clothes we don't wear anymore
        after a fashion

Our flight,
  rising up from the dead of desert night
    —brightly lit Phoenix

Surrounded by mountains —
   can't get over
  how fragile the desert feels

No Saguaro cacti up here —
   hard to climb
  with your hands in the air

Penciling in
        South-of-Phoenix property lines
  —Ponderosa pines

Fated, the time we'll arrive…
   this road we're on leads to one place
    —Tombstone

The O.K. Corral,
  click,click… couple of shots… got us!
    —camera man

Having flown away,
        they left behind a nestful
            of snow — wintry days

Muffled drumming
        getting lost in snowy silence
                —woodpecker Christmas

A giant snoring —
        though winter woods sound asleep,
                woodpecker's awake

Over the windows,
        letting in all the light — awning
                        of icicles

Nothing corresponds
        with its last known location
    —our buried mailbox

Overcast New Year's Day sky —
        in the air, something
                about to happen

A Persistent Tug

Dedication

To You, who,
   when we're pushing too much
      go on ahead... pulling for us

Bolting through the door,
   lightning on a leash — poodle
                    enthusiasm

Muzzle nuzzling
   crusty snow — poodle pulls out
            a frosted donut!

Neighboring woodland
                temporarily wetland
   —January thaw

Pond ice platform
      up where the surface used to be
            —rushes for pillars

Through thickness of fog
   (don't tell anyone)   — I looked
         right into the sun!

Weekend — things to do
  and time enough left to rest
    eyes on the full moon

News of a friend's death —
      bright sphere of light from beyond
        closed kitchen curtains

By the time you've heard
  a car's whoosh above the wind,
  you're dead — the blind bend

Lamp light left behind —
      dark adapting eyes, stars start
        refilling the sky

Fog engulfed —
    the winding road to home a string
  of educated guesses

Above the windbreak
    the two neighboring spruces
  carry the same curve

Having viewed the falls —
          contented souls trickle on
    back down the mountain

How our shadows leapt!
        crossing from the realm
    of one street lamp to the next

Shining
    through the crystalline makeup
      of each snowflake — a little sun

Blown down from atop
    the truck just ahead — my own
            personal snowstorm

Toenails click-clicking,
    dogs can't let sleeping folks lie
        —Saturday mornings

Windstorm's aftermath —
    swept into little piles,
        evergreen's sheddings

The Bird Family
    —its empty nest possessed by
        the crook of a tree

Tinsel from Christmas
    fringes a bird's nest — Easter
        around the corner

Crocuses come up
    and every so often,
    a spray of snowdrops

Wet late winter snow
delivers a crushing blow
      —crocus comeuppance

First day of spring —
   the flowering plants catalog
      dog-eared to dogwood

Appears
    to disappear —
spring, in-a-hurry-to-evaporate snow

One whoosh of the wind,
   they're off in a whirl —
      a few flighty snowflakes

Nagging me awake —
    snooze alarm... the insistent
     cawing of a crow

70

Early morning ducks
        spooked by the broken silence,
    scold me for my sin

Caught in the middle
        of their mating ritual —
    mallards taking flight

At the tip-top of a tall tree,
        one crow... one blink...
            thin air perches there

Snow from wires
    paints broken lines across the road
        —detour at springtime

Night drive, on a bridge
    at the edge of a small town,
    sounds of friends — peepers!

Gravity! in time,
        glass, and all that's seen through it
    get bent a little

Splashes... ripples spread
   out from the ditch through the dark
   —rains, amphibians

Couple of cowbirds
   perched together — East and West
      on the weathervane

Storm... sanctuary under spruce
         —wind chimes
      tuned to Kyoto's temple bells

The influence
   of a wild wind —
umbrella gets carried away!

Viewed behind the veil
         of clouds swiftly sailing by —
               half moon, half hidden

By the time I'd turned
back around — a band of clouds
made off with the moon!

Pond's perimeter —
beaver on patrol — tell-tale
thuh-thunks and splashes

Dawn, each blade of grass
carries a dewdrop
of a different color

Leaping by moonlight
over surface of the sea —
waves of ecstasy

Green-aqua-gold
inner curves of breaking waves
—Caribbean colors

Behind closed eyelids
            waves of the Caribbean
        instantly replayed

About-face prayer...
    beeline for the boat — shark seen
        first time snorkeling

"Shark!" I tried to shout,
    but the word got swallowed up
        —my snorkeling tube

Without a photo —
        just another fish story
        to the islanders

Our flotation mats aimed head on...
            full speed... Smack!... Smack!
        collision kisses!

Cutting-edge construction
   leveled in nothing flat
      —minds blown by high winds

Hurricane behind
      the island checkered with blue —
         St. Thomas roof tarps

No problems out here —
      all dissolve in one vast
                  saltwater solution

Rocking and rolling,
   walking around on sea legs
            —first days back on land

Mud-brown, mossy green —
   camouflaged though you may be...
      Bullfrog, you've been seen!

Rototilled earth... percolates
　　—gopher's out of garden
　　　　　　　experience

In the exact same spot
　　　sitting — Bullfrog, is that
　　　　　　your favorite rock?

Choruses in all kinds of keys,
　　　scores of birdsongs
　　—spring is in full swing

Birds in the branches,
　　　overheard, from overhead,
　　　　　cheep conversation

Hailstones hammering
　　　metal rooftop overhead
　　　　—all hairs stand on end

Not a sign of fight
 or flight in their eyes — deer just watching
          cars roar by

Gazing into the eyes of a deer
           —distance between us
                    disappears

Rustling through brush —
      nearby deer under cover
   of the new moon night

An opening
   between branches where clouds had been
      —full moon flooding in

With gusto we greet
      each bat, "Bon Appetit!"
   —buggy about the bog

Robins land with chirps
   and splashes of sunlight — dew drops
                 from tree branches

Together, they just click —
    so many different
        rhythms of crickets

While you're at it, please
    give them some big ones for me,
        mountain-hugging clouds!

Family emergency…
    night drive — mountains
  climbing out of the fog

Sunrise on the day after her death,
    flooded with light,
          the evergreen

Survived… summer of much rain
    —cactus set outside
        sunny day last May

First frost, but wait! whew!
  —my wife remembered
        to move the cactus inside

Weeks of waiting...
      Sun, won't you come and coax
gladiolas into bloom?

Morning shower —
    through the bathroom window,
      what a watery world!

Foliage through mist
  —holding pastels, hills make good
    all around easels!

Maples through windows...
    reds, yellows, greens, oranges
      —a jumble out there!

Equine clip-clop,
        canine commentary — crisp
                autumn cacophony

Neighbor's puppies left out late...
        lightning! —on and off—
                their frantic faces

Spectacular autumn colors —
        facial muscles
                frozen in a grin

Wild colors of sunrise —
        passively fall leaves
        picking them all up

Charcoal clouds
        underlit by city lights
        —airborne surrealism

Autumn —
  chameleon vines full of leaves
      turn into red brick background

Their pull is strong —
  leashed dogs sniffing out trails of
          phantom animals

Sunrise wastes no time
      brightening the countryside
  —gold October leaves

Drainage ditch
  loaded with leaves and rain — whirlpool
          bubbles at the bend

New York night, air flight —
      light bulbs below flickering
  —obstacles unseen

Red setting sun looms
        over Texas horizon —
the enormousness

Safe behind the Alamo's outer walls —
    a canal full of gold
                        fish

Half circle
    of a different color —
gill of a goldfish stands out

Border town,
    a persistent tug… little, big eyes…
        —"Mister, buy chicle?"

Driver's lookout —
    orange sun fills the rearview mirror,
        full moon ahead

Red tide: with each wave,
    another fish rolling in
                its watery grave

Bluffside,
   barnacle-encrusted root-ball of tree
               —far reach of the sea

Rising tide —
     people busy keeping cars
  from becoming submarines

It creeps up on you —
     folks hustle to reclaim
        belongings from the sea

Folks, that's close enough!
    egret retreats from jetty
  to a nearby bluff

Scarecrow alone
    in freshly harvested fields
  still standing sentinel

All In An Instant

Dedication

To Eternal Love,
 whose Grace sheds light
        everywhere it radiates

October snow —
    making sure we know
        we're not in Texas anymore

Final fall courtin' call?
    the persevering pleas
        of a lone peeper

Thick crust of frost
        gets softened by ascending sun
    —things done by degrees

Deep oranges
    coming over forest floors
        —fall flings' afterglowings

Trees free of leaves —
    from edges of woods
  with ease one sees all the way through

Blades ablaze, brilliance in abundance —
behold the grades of gold
grasses!

The odd breeze pressing
for their release — finally,
a few flakes fly... freed!

Last night's snow
slowly letting go of the spruce tree
—sun-drenched and dripping

Wind and rain exposed —
what magic keeps this place so
full of foliage?

What luck!
falling into our laps amid maples
—light through yellow leaves

Connecting
   many little islands of marsh grass —
      massive mass of ice

Cloud-hugged horizon...
      romantic expanse of sky...
   kissed by crescent moon

Persuasive power
      of the wind — no sweat getting
         the hemlock to give

Seed fluff of cattails,
      growing cold... left-standing sticks...
         ashes on incense

Long lines forming across the sky
   —clouds receive
               light from the morning sun

Just dawning on me,
     last night's dream — unearthly light
        at the break of day

Surprise snow and ice —
     the forecaster seems to be
        slipping a little

How long can what goes up stay up?
     —wind blowing snowing
        horizontal

Storm clouds collect —
     my cup of tea contributing
        steam to the system

Spaces between snow clouds
     until sun-up unseen
        —hot pink highlighting

Imprismed cloud
    divulges all — color components
      of full moon's light

Cold rain —
  not complaining to the Management,
     this thanks-giver shivers

Overnight chill —
    intense orange sunrise
  warming me on the inside

Thermometer
    mercury not moving
 —another messenger, shot!

Deep night — in stillness,
    awareness assuming
  enormous proportions

Right up from the ground,
        with grasses along the stream
            —ice crystals growing

Pet-stop — at first tree,
    surrounded by skittering
        sounds of landing sleet

Bank of a turn —
    geese scramble... a new order
        into their formation

Two crows, quiet, top of a tree
    out of mist, geese
        honking their heads off

Geese — the two second fiddles
        exchange positions...
    chevron shuffling

Foothills —
    rainfall-filled basin below,
    roads awash in the overflow

A fine white line —
   where snow-powdered mountains end
      and morning mist begins

Sky half-overcast —
   where clouds stop,
    exploring eyes... step... off into space

By street lamp's light
   streaming over the big white screen
                  falling snow's shadows

Gorging
   on twigs, leaves, rain, and melting snow
      —fattening-up waterfall

Filled out waterfall, floating mist...
   snow-melt drips
                  at the middle of this

Spotted in the woods —
  one hundred and one bark-muffled,
    snow-spattered trees

Winter ritual —
    skiers fling themselves
        at the feet of fallen snow

Following too close
      precipitates pile-ups
  —back-to-back nor'easters

Out-in-the-road doe —
  stalwart, waiting... for her fawn
            to catch up and cross

Holding such promise,
  any moment might explode —
    New Year's fireworks!

Linked to a long chain
　　of snow-capped little islands
　　　　—plumes of steam mid-stream

Working overtime —
　　through overcast dawn... street lamps
　　　　at their posts, glare on

After a brief thaw —
　　　by full moon's light, the pond looks
　　　　almost all patched up

Sent sprawling across yards of ice —
　　　crab apple's shadow
　　　　　　by full moonlight

Still up at dawn,
　　　　high over clouded horizon
　　—moon outshines them all

Screen of light snowfall —
    powerful, piercing... heron's
      scream from the unseen

Sunrise — standing just so,
    spruce tree in all its glory
        ...with a halo!

Each slight move broadcasts
    beaver's culvert location
      —stream's frozen silence

Rabbit tracks in snow —
   the only hint
     anything's hopping around here

Pulled and pulled across
    sparkling expansive sky
      —star-gazing dog-walk

February —
              bright full moon-lit night,
cracking ice, honking geese... sing peace

Shroud over the lake
              from which these islands arise
                            —mist and mystery

Climbing out
          at the fog-covered far side of the lake
                                      —phantom mountain

Clouds, a range themselves,
          appear to mimic the mountains
                            behind their backs

Broken sound barrier...
          there! an orange spark... repairs
                              to northern night sky

Morning snow — distant duck's call
answered by cawing
hidden local crow

Mouse-nibbled pages —
   long winter stash of dog food
          shelved behind the books

Rooftop sun —
     at waterspouts' tips, drips,
          wind-chilled icicle haywire

Spring's parade frozen
           mid-mountain cascade...
       waters masquerade... as ice

Day's steady drizzle...
   dampening night... softened footsteps...
           deepening silence

...turns to freezing rain —
      temperatures plummet
        this side of the summit

Spruce trees wide in the rain —
     but under weight of wet snow,
       umbrellas closed

Flocks in flux,
  influx of seabirds inland
  —rapid snow-melt, flash flooding

Fine rain — specks of light in the dark —
     peepers' sounds mixed in
           amidst the mist

Sprinkling, sparkling spray —
     particles of moon-lamp light
          ...ricochet!

A wayward little whirlwind —
    sparse snowfall
       caught up in its world

Their carvings
     echo curvings of the earth —
contour plowings, in-plane view

First beach-walk —
  all tensions recede
     beside the turbulence of the sea

White caps, within range, brought
    by lighting from the beach
      —visible wavelengths

Extended presence
    of the city's fluorescence
—surf's unearthly glow

Through one cracked eyelid,
    slit in cloudy horizon
      —fraction of sunrise

Swimming in satisfaction —
   undiminished
                appetite for ocean

Viewing the ocean
   over breakfast — over easy
      gentle wave breaks

From wave tops spill drops of light
   —taking them all in,
              surf is raining sun

Its dark foreboding,
   not-fully-defined form;
      beachfront, brewing — a storm

Storm at sea — charred clouds,
  singed mist left behind, lightning
          bolts into the blue

Gale-gliding seagulls
　　　racing strings of sea-storm clouds
　　　　　—measured in knots... tied!

After the big storm
　　　sitting alone on the beach
　　　　　—a complete conch shell

Skin seared red from so much sun
　　　sleeping sitting up...
　　　　　ah, but such seashells!

Between pelicans,
　　　between pelicans and ocean,
　　　　　—only inches

Waves! unwavering —
　　　the in-line formation
　　　　　of in-flight pelicans

Pelican with dark wing tips
dives into the water
for fish... and dip!

Clouds hanging back —
lavender network reflects,
mingles with aqua blue

The fetching blonde
—while she flirts, her Rottweiler
goes digging up the beach

Drifting off...
in surround sound, ocean waves
serenading us to sleep

Wind, dogs, frogs —
their whistling, howling, peeping
prelude to a storm

Planting completed —
    the following day's rain
        watering new willows

Days of falling rain —
    all in an instant, the air
        cleared by songbird's trill

Absorbing? Imagine this —
    mist hanging
    over the weeping willows

Forsythia shines —
    its unruly new growth shoots…
        yellow fireworks!

The culprit setting
    the woodpile on fire
  —sidelit by the sun

Utility pole —
    top of it lit by a few stray
      first rays of day

Hushed, You Can Hear It

Dedication

To the Great Energy
that's humming at the heart
of everything

Small-town springtime's plentiful frills —
lots of yellow
double daffodils

With wild grasses —
a refined fuchsia tulip
just seems to fit in

Sun catchers flicker
green, silver, gold... wind flutters
left-alone grasses

As breezes blow, so the part goes...
naturally wavy
untrimmed grass

Dandelions, who was that
unmasked man — who chopped
your little heads off?

With cricket chorus,
       echo-filtered through the woods,
          blends mower's motor

In a flash, arcing
       the length of the chain-link fence —
          crackling lightning

Working with whipping winds —
  waves of rain
     sweep up hailstone-littered sidewalks

Deep post-downpour breaths —
  storm spent... heavenly scent
         of earth is in the air

Eyes left on Hilldale Road —
    glistening gold, mist
       in after-storm sunlight

Hats off!
        dry heavenly humor —
    heads moistened by invisible mist

Horse chestnut with one hell of a hull —
    threatened hedgehog
                rolled into one

Mother's Day — the night
    brightened by constellations
        blossoms by moonlight

Rabbit's burial —
    this Mother's Day we honor
            comings and goings

Over, under, through —
    two dogs and their walker freed
            from tangled leashes

Wind bellows;
    not one to be bullied, brick building
                refuses to budge

Pre-nightfall, post-rain —
        everything sparkling
    in the in-between

Dewdrops in sun, shine
   some stand out, bright... the rest recede...
           soft green, glowing

Just swept up
    and over a speeding truck —
    dragonfly recovering

Airplane, stirring flight-pattern change
        into storm-cloud, banks...
    winding vapor trails

Goose sounds the all clear...
    rain-rinsed atmosphere...
    sun-bathed street's a stream — of light

Sun's dazzling flames
    thrown here from the horizon
        —burnt-reddish spruce tree

Short on dunk, long on spunk—
    dachshund on a roll
        with the big basketball

Bird scats through a couple of bars
    cage walls of water —
        rain's steady beat

Nudged by last night's rain,
    this morning the crab apple
        begins to blossom

Creek bubbles over its banks —
   flowering crab apple bursts
                  into bloom

Freshly mown
    pink petal-strewn lawn — crab apple's
                elegant negligence

More pink petals
     found far afield — crab apple's
           wide sphere of influence

Our race the sun won...
    I squint for the finished line
         —mowing in the dark

Bicycling
        came to a stop... focus broken,
    now fixed on birdsong

Once within earshot,
     pulled into pure paradise
  —warble of wood thrush

Distant bird calls — this
        is as close as one can come...
            without trespassing

Music composition
        way over my head —
                canopy of birdcall

Columbine in rain,
        taking a direct hit, falls
                to petal pieces

Slower layer of clouds —
        my mind keeps blowing it
                the opposite way!

Recent rain dripping
        between footsteps in the dark
                a random rhythm

Wisps of cloud spreading out
     slowly dissipate
  Whoa! the vastness of space!

With starlit backdrop —
      a strand of cloud softly shines
          by crescent moon's light

Fireflies set off
     twilight's yellow twinkling
        —buttercup background

Hushed, you can hear it —
     the hummingbird's hovering
    whisper of wingsong

Morning rounds —
     hummingbird carries the tune
        to each of the red zinnias

Solstice! hottest of pinks
    present themselves to summer
        —opening day!

With a charge, lightning leads the way
    thunder rip-roaring
            right behind it

Street lamp blinking —
    half-blinded, the electric eye
        in a lightning storm

Now and again
    you get glimpses of a ghost town
    —stark nighttime lightning

Hunkered down with dogs,
    group hug in the thunderstorm
        —bracing, embracing

In you flit — leave
  your little wing-motor running, and split,
                                  hummingbird

World traveler —
    chapel full of well-wishers
              bids her bon voyage

Dangling
    twenty feet post-take-off
—already-in-formation geese

Hot, hazy night —
    eyes climb through smoky orange
      tunnel to the full moon

After a dry spell —
    central channel of the stream
      filled by the full moon

Applauding through aspen leaves,
through cattails taking a bow,
—cool wind waves

Spilled into the pond —
ride of the drunken driver
ends up in the drink

Each crunch punctuates
our back porch conversation
—apple-munching deer

Crepuscular cuisine —
rabbits, deer... make morsels
of my moss roses

Lights pierce, winds disperse
post-precipitation mists
—passing motorists

Master rolls over...
opportunity! dog dives
beneath the blankets!

Mist over the marsh
    picks up cloudless, starry sky
        —glowing in the dark

Eyes sharp this morning
    saw sky with a jagged edge
        —ragged ridge of spruce

Cloudy dawn's bronze glow —
    out from cover of cattails,
        flash of a goldfinch

Crowds of Queen Anne's Lace...
    off by themselves, a couple
        of Shasta daisies

Outages on Earth,
    liquid spills from the sky
    —lightning jumping with juice

Queen Anne's Lace laden
  with a luminescence
    —full moon's giving presence

Soft thoughts,
    absorbing peace of this place —
wisps of mist, whispers of crickets

Barest of breezes —
  almost imperceptibly,
    bushes' branches sway

Clouds diffract double
    —beside myself over this
      view of two full moons

Begging snack scraps,
    pier pigeons — toes missing,
      fishing-line-embedded feet

Seagull, on a spree,
  tries taking off — shopping
              bag's handle in its beak

Morro Bay estuary —
  plovers' eggs... protected here
                  from breakers

Tide going out —
            in the eye of a whirlpool,
    rock's reappearance

Crowded rock... groans —
      as one seal shifts, the rest refit
                  the puzzle pieces

Small rock
      balancing, one seal
          caresses the other with a flipper

Incoming tide —
     remaining harbor seal
          wave-swept from favorite rock

Churning surf —
   picked-up shells and rocks tumble, settle
                    and roll jingling

Fog wafting into the cove —
     time on vacation,
              secluded dreamworld

Waves split... sweeping curves...
     complete wraparound — outskirts
                    of little islands

Migration!
     around a wall of headwind,
     Monarch butterfly tacking

Japanese garden —
    enormous stretch to reach
        each steep half-moon-bridge step

Dad's hand poised to assist
    —daughter determined
        to climb it on her own

Japanese garden — the trees
        in all those old screens
    were not stylized!

Golden Gate Park —
    Sundays, holidays, like clockwork,
        "impromptu drumming"

Luggage crammed with souvenirs —
    we pass a freight train
        on parallel tracks

Solitary spruce —
      look again… birds by the branchful
                        are blending in

Wind tugs
    clouds' piled cargo of warm color —
          vermilion sunrise

Cloud drifts
    filling the gap… barely overlapping
                 nearly a full moon

Autumn color change —
      elms in rain dripping leaves
              deepening liquid gold

Cuddled with poodle,
      bathed in beams from the full moon
      —simple luxury

Stretch of lit highway —
    frozen in forest's shadows,
        separated deer

Tick... tick... freezing rain...
   day off work... not! a moment to lose —
                        home projects!

Plover's peeps
   take on a tone of protest —
           season's first pelting of sleet

Wrapped in silence
   'til the gift gets opened — chimes spill out
           strings of ringings

Each stride into evening fog
      more deeply enfolded
      —moving stillness

Through a crack in traffic
     cardinal just flits — bright red
           flash... of brake lights!

Missing Not A Thing

Dedication

To You, Who, holding all things,
withholding nothing,
       are really something

Airborne — lost...
  sun's rays comb the clouds... finally find
                              our hidden heaven

Cloudless sky,
                 what shadows are these?
     undulating offshore manta rays

Fronds drawn together —
         overlapping, cross-hatching,
               shade trees fill in sky

Sun-softened, I slip
         smoothly through their silkiness
           —calm evening waters

Orange-pink sunset
  bouncing from clouds to waves, and sand
                    soaking it up

Off waterfront walls,
      echoing — loud-laughing
            Sunday morning seagulls

Night storm...
      light show far out to sea
—fourteenth floor front row balcony seat

Flashes going off;
      clouds light up from the inside
          —in pastels, pulsing

After Grandma's funeral,
        the endless procession
            of ocean's waves

Swell coming in...
      splash subsides, slips away...
        buried by subsequent waves

Outgrowing the old,
      mollusk lays down a deposit
           on a new home

Landing in the fog,
      haloes everywhere...
      airport light bulb heaven!

Bare lilac branches
  red sunrise-silhouetted
          —missing not a thing

Viewing the lilac
      from various vantage points
      —all the odd angles

Heaven's happenings —
      snowflakes fall to earth
  in great crystalline clusters

Welcoming the New Year —
      sparkle dance of lamplight,
        surfaces of snow

Drizzly thaw — water
      gurgles at ground level... drips
          from all that's tall

After the ice storm,
      caught up in crystal treetops —
    sun rose pink clear through

Sunlight! appearance of fire
        through the trees — crackling
              icicles

Wings red, wave overhead...
      duck couple — valentines
        day dawns upon them

Cloud-free horizon —
    from still dark valley, eyes rise
        to shining highlands

Barking their heads off —
    dogs introduced to stranger
        snowman in the yard

Snowman must present
    a startling silhouette —
        skunk scent at sunup

Warm day — drawn to the snowman
        just in time to catch
          his head falling off

In with the breath,
  returned to the sky with a sigh —
    orange crescent moon

Branches, wires spark my quest
for full view of this
pieced-together moon

Luscious, but who'd run off
        with the moon? cantaloupe
                sliced to a sliver

Sky opened up at dawn —
        between sun and myself,
                softest of rains shines

Cloudbursts, sunlight reveals
        the secret sparkling spots —
                gentle rain drops

With that sound beating
    —hands down— I surrender!
                —caught in a downpour

So full, the rising moon
        seems to have gotten stuck
                between two spruce trees

Sun, shown on each face,
    flashes as it's reflected
        off flipping snowflakes

A shame to show up
    her majesty — the Full Moon,
    humble hint of sea

Sea water swirls
    in pools among jetty rocks
        —natica nestled

Wave-washed morning mind
    skipping across... timeless trails
        of left-behind rocks

Whipped up by the wind
    to a stiff, half-frozen froth
        —saltwater daffy

Disintegrating
as it's blown across white sand —
ghost beach tumblefoam

Just off the ocean,
wind finds flimsy resistance —
rattling railings

Beachcomber wind —
raking up the cape,
leaves rippled patterns in the sand

While we wait, wind
makes it whole again — cloud-split,
massive orange moon

Which of us looks more curious?
a lone, nearby seagull
facing me

Winter crossing spring's border —
　　field's edge littered
　　　　with broken crocuses

No longer pinned down —
　　surviving snowdrops emerge
　　　　fully camouflaged

Stopped, just standing here,
　　feeling rushing over me
　　　　first whiff of sea air

With my wife's blessings
　　I carry on... long-term love affair
　　　　　　with ocean

Darkened balcony —
　　wave sounds swell over sea wall
　　　　inundating me

Just inside sea wall,
   mom scoops up squirt, scoots off beach
      —low-level sandstorm

Wave-stirred whirlpools,
      little holes drilled in dry sand
   —water fizzes in

Released in waves,
      lodes of gas escape the sand
   —groups of tiny geysers

Wind, must you keep it
   just out of my reach? seagull's
         feather souvenir

Retracing beach steps...
   fresh tracks with mine intertwined
      —gull's been following

There's wind in it yet —
　　birthday balloon bouquet blown,
　　　　bouncing up the beach

Winter glove washed up —
　　a single golden seashell
　　　　in the palm of it

Imagine... just who
　　might have had a hand in this
　　　　glove found with shell held?

Sunset spilling out —
　　splash of a fisherman's cast
　　　　added to the drink

Curtains! outside them all is lost...
　　consumed by morning sun
　　　　　　　　at Sea Bright

Specks next to so much —
  sky, sand, sea — ladybug perched,
    oceanside, on me

Deficiency-free —
　beached shell filled with small shells, sand
　　and bubbling sea

Sand-stranded horseshoe crab turns
　from seaweed green
　　　to color of beach — peach

Ocean waves at night;
　the image still with me —
　　full moon provides the flash

Wave formation —
　　　inside each curl before cresting,
　　gloss from full moon

Cylindrical hole
　bored in boulder — wave chute formed
　　　　by jetty's juttings

Animate object —
   stiff wind sets metal can lid
      upright and rolling

End of an enormous meal —
   dessert's frosting furnished
          by a full moon

One boardwalk street lamp
   glowing orange in daylight
     —early marigold

Web of evidence
   dredged from the deep — fresh prints
     place high tide at the scene

Glint of gold glancing
     off windows across the way
    —skyscraper sunrise

Surprising spring heat —
   resounding through the marshland,
     gurglings of ducks

Frigid Atlantic
   flow tide catches me crossing
     barely a sandbar

Wind-borne beach debris —
   just to see, I'm forced to clean
    salt spray from glasses

Beachcomber's cache
  of the day displayed: all scallop shells
      —same, different

First, before sunning,
  I seek gully's protection
    —beach sand-blasting wind

As one approaches
 pigeons flee nests, and from new perches,
   coo, "Yoo hoo!"

The Scotch pine
      looking fuzzier than usual
      through twilight drizzle

Cold-to-the-core downpour —
  whit of whiteness runs through each
                 long drawn-out drop

Forsythia blooms
       drop atop dandelions —
             April lawn yellows

May Day! flowering crab
  dropping its petals already
            —El Niño

Blamed for a series
        of punishing rainstorms
    that bad boy — El Niño

Getting fidgety,
        I'm informed by the waiter —
            it wasn't decaf

Rail-split raindrops glide
    underside... collide... re-fuse
        to finish falling

What?!   What time?!   Where...
    in the world am I?! — hotel,
            early, fire alarm

Right off a live plant
        sparrow plucked some tender leaves
            for added padding

Golf course-engulfing,
  rain-swollen, serpentine stream —
    green within its grasp

Plumes of rain falling,
  rays shoot down — cloudburst failing
    to dampen the sun

Summer saltwater
    flipped a couple of clam shells
      straight up in the air

Into the protected area
    venture two
        unendangered ducks

Windy at the beach —
    seagull feather found sanded down
      close to the quill

Standing surrounded
        by dozens of gull prints
  —sense of community

Wooden ramps to the beach
    left hanging way out over
       eroding coastline

Hardly out of sand —
    tops of a few rocks — jetty's
       almost history

Tidal legacy —
  rich settlement of seaweed
    resurfacing rocks

A bigger honking V's never met these eyes
    —goose bumps
            cover this guy

Three gulls
  on three still-standing, off-shore piles —
    where the pier used to end

An Unperturbed Path

Dedication

To You through whose guidance
entanglements unwind
— path to peace of mind

With ropes of seaweed,
   tug-of-warring with ocean —
                    mussel-bound jetty

Running, not flying —
   gull escapes getting tagged "it"
                    by human toddler

Compounded poundings —
      offshore thunderstorm fills in
            lulls between the waves

Inches from ocean,
         down-sized by sovereign sea
            —overthrown ruler

That goat,
never far from its favorite horse, grazing
            —best barnyard buds!

Told, "too soon for dolphins,"
    wistfully I scan the sea —
        two bottlenose!

Acting camouflaged,
    observing tourist traffic —
        spotted local cat

Square window, chute through clouds —
    long box of sunlight
        delivered to the ground

Lobbed green tennis ball…
    Out! among the fallen fruit
        — crab-apple court yard

Parading prize rock
    retrieved from the swimming hole
        —dog daring diver

Box canyon —
   at the opening, pieces
of corrugated coastline

Trying them all on —
   hummingbird finds each foxglove
      a full-filling fit

Nesting jay
   raids bike rider's helmet-free head
    —moving violation

Diver's mask, flippers,
    vanish into foam — little
     hot tub explorer

With autumn backdrop,
bright green bursts in through the window
       climbing ivy

Burnt-orange maple
   sandwiched between brick buildings
      —relit at lunch break

Out, hugging the overhang —
                     I notice my wife
                  doesn't have to duck

At the summit
         she asks whether arriving climbers
               knew there were stairs

Past the last passageway —
         rock, lizard, and I come
                  face to face to face

Which local sees us
         reach the top of Morro Rock?
      —a lounging lizard!

Between mountains and clouds,
  setting sun's light... extinguishes
                 distinctions

Motion detected —
      eyefuls of stars floodlit
            into obscurity

Gentle, abused dog
    snaps, but won't clamp down — asking
            to be left alone

Human form ahead —
      double-taking buck
    gauging danger with a gasp

Spinning right around,
  wild-eyed buck blows the scene —
          building head of steam

Synchronous swarm,
      signature of migrating swallows
     look — flourishes!

Cool-jet jacuzzi,
         trough beset by river rocks
  —rapid shooting me!

Faces of snowflakes —
      full moon beams us sparkling
        into the New Year

Warehouse — puppy bounding about
      stacks of rugs, rolls
            of linoleum

Night walk down our road
      past the misted-over marsh
      —familiar unknown

Warm road — packed snow thaws...
    slow-going nighttime drive-through —
          hood winked out in fog

On steep, winding roads
    almost lost it — waning moon
        looking lopsided

Puff of warm breath
    through the car door's frozen keyhole —
        commute-resolute

Accumulating cumulus clouds —
    days indoors...
lost track of the sun

Jet's out-of-synch strobes
    flicker in flight, wobble straight
        across the cosmos

Tunnel vision —
    in the yard, dug, one final hole
        for the departed mole

By crescent moon's light —
  winds comb through the weathered brush,
          search for signs of life

Squirrel's nonchalance
    crossing frigid drainage ditch,
              one thin branch — its bridge

Marsh ice comes up
    with one heck of a crack:
          howling wind — hissing grasses

Cloudy minus ten degrees of open sky
          —light leaks
                    from crack of dawn

Mild dawn —
    up and down the spruce,
          varied perches, pitches of phoebes

Storm clouds
  over crowded parking lot — seagulls
    lighten the atmosphere

Double taken,
  mistaken for marshmallows
    —fence post's melting snow caps

Spots before my eyes —
    ladybugs' fuel efficient
        new light bulb lodging

Softly, distinctly —
      you can hear each slush-drop land
          among the grasses

Wheee! where muskrat found
    snow-hidden ice — pre-paw-print,
                long linear tracks

Kid-filled pool —
loving couple in the jacuzzi
ducking cannonballs

Through cracked car window
at stream's country crossing — fresh
voice of a peeper

Drawn here by swift winds —
where none had been, wisp-edged clouds
being air-brushed in

Waves just miss its feet —
from full-speed piping plover,
an uplifting peep

Driftwood resembles
crab claw on which it rests —
prosthesis in a pinch?

Tossed out by the sea,
     shipped misshapen back to shore
          —abandoned frisbee

Plastic golf ball,
     water hazard to sand trap,
          to shore from sea — missed tee

One jackknife,
     I'd be in a terrific jam
     —sandwiched between bread trucks

Bicyclist sighted —
     critters scatter... fade
          into bordering forest

Intruder alert!
     —with each white tuft fluffed, dozens
          of grazing deer flee

Turtle's plunge into deepening shadows
—just-drifting-off stream,
a wake

Wind, a ways away
      arises, leaves announce
            its local arrival

Post-Easter
   post office early bird picks up his
          chirping box of chicks

Whole flock taking off —
   seagulls bigger than the boy
      bearing down on them

Waves break
   through layers of mist — surf emerges
      awash in pure whiteness

Solidifying
   from a different dimension —
      girl through the mist

Thunder's third warning
off darkening beach, stampede
elephant raindrops

Dream state, shifting
car into gear — bedside alarm
jolts me to a stop

At stoplight,
gift of prior-passed-driver passed on —
a suggestive yawn

From between car wheels —
chipmunk, alive! moves four feet,
highway to haven

Bicycle's brakes squeal —
porcupine plodding along
an unperturbed path

Hearing my gearing,
    deer hoofs it over the road
        —an eight-click crossing

At last roadside second —
    wild turkey's crash dash
        for wooded cover

If anyone comes
    anywhere close — sunning geese
        honk beside the road

Earthly oddity
    with other-worldly weirdness
        —a veery's double voice

Whistle-warning,
    releasing steam, or mimicking?
        blue jay's bold-note blast

Keeping five goslings
  swimming close — constantly on
      parental patrol

As the heron flies —
  it points up the stream
    meandering through the marsh

Beyond the reaches
  of ordinary speeches —
      high-flutin' wood thrush

Showering all day
  rinses all the gray away
    —sparkling sunset

Pooch plunging
  into overgrown grasses,
  pivots — now he's chasing me!

At the beach, heads turn
to follow a real looker —
stripe-winged dragonfly!

Hummingbird: "So slow
you humans go... C'mon! Let's
refill those feeders!"

Clipped-wing cockatiel... squawks,
walks, three long rooms away —
family voices

What's come over me?
—one wind-borne whiff of roses
from across the yard

Deer's precise timing —
highway rush hour crossing,
never breaking stride

Lawn care truck ahead —
    each escaped leaf's unique
       twirling trajectory

Stone wall caving in
    half-hidden inner chambers
       woodchuck's checking out

Maple serves
    as key source of calories
—chipmunks stuffing their faces

Give her a wide berth!
    snapper digs in, bears down
      —turtles' egg-laying turf

Back road mobile home —
    from its yard, the shrill alarm
      of captive peacocks

At stream top eye-level —
   puff of milkweed floats
   up on its filaments

Nighttime storm clouds blowing over,
nearly stepped-on skunk
—saving their sprays

Aching for a stretch —
horse pounds the ground in protest
on tortuous trails

Sunlight angling
over road and into woods
—fern scene, glowing green

Making their meters
remaining daylight displays
—spruces' tall lit tops

Finishing things up —
spurred on by a newfound
openness to closure